MW00327871

Novels for Students, Volume 30

Project Editor: Sara Constantakis Rights Acquisition and Management: Leitha Etheridge-Sims, Sari Gordon, Aja Perales, Jhanay Williams Composition: Evi Abou-El-Seoud Manufacturing: Drew Kalasky

Imaging: John Watkins

Product Design: Pamela A. E. Galbreath, Jennifer Wahi Content Conversion: Katrina Coach Product Manager: Meggin Condino © 2010 Gale, Cengage Learning

For product information and technology assistance, contact us at **Gale Customer Support, 1-800-877-4253.**

For permission to use material from this text or product, submit all requests online at **www.cengage.com/permissions.**

Further permissions questions can be emailed to **permissionrequest@cengage.com** While every effort has been made to ensure the reliability of the information presented in this publication, Gale, a part of Cengage Learning, does not guarantee the accuracy of the data contained herein. Gale accepts no payment for listing; and inclusion in the publication of any organization, agency, institution, publication, service, or individual does not imply endorsement of the editors or publisher. Errors brought to the attention of the publisher and verified to the satisfaction of the publisher will be corrected in future editions.

Gale
27500 Drake Rd.
Farmington Hills, MI, 48331-3535

ISBN-13: 978-0-7876-8687-1
ISBN-10: 0-7876-8687-5
ISSN 1094-3552

This title is also available as an e-book.
ISBN-13: 978-1-4144-4946-3
ISBN-10: 1-4144-4946-1
Contact your Gale, a part of Cengage Learning sales
representative for ordering information.

Printed in the United States of America
1 2 3 4 5 6 7 13 12 11 10 09

The Little Prince

Antoine de Saint-Exupéry

1943

Introduction

The children's story *The Little Prince*, by the French author and aviation pioneer Antoine de Saint-Exupéry, was first published by Reynal & Hitchcock in the original French as *Le Petit Prince* in 1943. Also in 1943, the same publisher brought out an English-language version, translated by Katherine Woods, under the title *The Little Prince*. As of 2008, it is available in a 2000 edition published by Harvest Books, translated by Richard Howard.

The Little Prince tells the story of an encounter between an aviator whose airplane has crashed in the desert and an enigmatic visitor from another planet, the little prince of the title. The little prince's account of his journey to Earth via other planets and his impressions of the inhabitants becomes an allegory of human nature. An allegory is a representation of an abstract or spiritual meaning through concrete or material forms. The novel's themes include spiritual decay and the importance of establishing bonds of love and responsibility with other beings.

The novel is part of a French literary tradition of allegorical fantasies, of which the novel *Candide* (1759), by the eighteenth-century French author and philosopher Voltaire, is one of the best-known examples. In France, *The Little Prince* confirmed Saint-Exupéry's reputation as a great writer on aviation whose works have deep moral and spiritual significance.

Elsewhere in the world, the novel was largely ignored by critics and academics in the decades following the author's death in 1944. However, this has not prevented the work becoming a great popular success with both adults and children across the world. It has become one of the most widely translated works of French literature.

Author Biography

The French author and aviator Antoine Jean Baptiste Marie Roger de Saint-Exupéry was born on June 29, 1900, in Lyon, France, into an aristocratic family. He was the third child of Count Jean de Saint-Exupéry, an insurance company executive, and his wife Marie de Fonscolombe de Saint-Exupéry. Count Jean died in 1904. In 1909, his widow moved with her children to live at the home of her aunt, the castle of Saint-Maurice-de-Rémens in Le Mans. Saint-Exupéry spent a happy childhood surrounded by his sisters and an extended family of aunts and cousins. His early interest in aviation was fuelled by family vacations taken near the airport at Bugey.

Saint-Exupéry was educated at Jesuit schools in Montgré and Le Mans and between 1915 and 1917 at a Catholic boarding school in Fribourg, Switzerland. He failed an examination to enter naval school and entered the École des Beaux-Arts to study architecture. After a short period of study he left in 1921 to begin military service. A turning point in Saint-Exupéry's life came when he was transferred to Strasbourg and later to Rabat in Morocco, as in both places he was able to take flying lessons. He received his pilot's license in 1922. During an assignment in Paris he had the first of a number of serious crashes.

Saint-Exupéry wanted to pursue a career in the

air force, but objections were raised by the family of his fiancée, Louise de Vilmorin. He agreed to take a job that the family arranged for him in a tile manufacturing firm, but he continued to fly in his spare time. De Vilmorin broke the engagement in 1923, whereupon Saint-Exupéry left the tile firm and took a variety of jobs. He had begun to write, and his first published work was a story called "L'Aviateur" ("The Aviator"), which appeared in a magazine called *Le Navire d'Argent* in 1926. Some of Saint-Exupéry's favorite themes are already visible in the story, including the experience of flying and how it contrasts with the society left behind.

In 1926 Saint-Exupéry took a job flying the mail over North Africa for a commercial airline company, Aéropostale. Two years later he became the director of the remote Cap Juby airfield in the Spanish Sahara, where he lived in an isolated wooden shack. He developed a deep love of the desert, which later formed the setting for his novels *The Little Prince* (1943) and *Citadelle* (1948; translated into English as *The Wisdom of the Sands*, 1950). He improved relations between the Spaniards and the Moors in the region and also voluntarily engaged in dangerous rescue missions, accomplishing the rescue of downed pilots, the recovery of a plane, and the exchange of pilots being held for ransom. His courage was recognized in 1929, when he was awarded the French Legion of Honor Award. His experiences at Aéropostale and Cap Juby are reflected in his semiautobiographical novel *Courrier Sud* (1929; translated as *Southern*

Mail, 1933).

Saint-Exupéry returned to France in 1928, and the following year he moved to South America to take up a post flying mail through the Andes for the Aeroposta Argentina Company. The occupation provided material for the novel that made his name, *Vol de Nuit* (1931; translated as *Night Flight*, 1932). The novel became an international bestseller, won the Prix Femina (a French literary prize) in 1931, and was adapted for film two years later (*Night Flight*, 1933).

Saint-Exupéry traveled on leave to France in 1931, bringing with him a widowed Argentinian author and artist named Consuelo Goómez Carrillo, whom he married in Grasse. The marriage was stormy, as Saint-Exupéry was often absent and had affairs. In her memoir of their marriage, discovered in 1999 and published as *The Tale of the Rose*, Consuelo wrote that she was the model for the character of the rose in *The Little Prince*.

While Saint-Exupéry was in France, he heard that he was without a job, as the Aeroposta Argentina Company had collapsed. He took a position piloting hydroplanes in Africa but lost it after nearly drowning in a crash. In 1934, he began working as a journalist, traveling to Moscow and Spain to write reports. In 1935, he crashed his plane in the North African desert while trying to break a speed record in a contest and nearly died from dehydration before being saved by a Bedouin. The experience is reflected in *Le Petit Prince* (*The Little Prince*) and in his collection of anecdotes, meditations, and memoirs titled *Terre des Hommes* (1939; translated as *Wind, Sand and Stars*, 1939). Saint-Exupéry wrote *Terre des Hommes* while convalescing from severe injuries resulting from his crashing his plane in Guatemala. It was awarded the Grand Prix du Roman of the Académie Française and the National Book Award in the United States 1939.

World War II broke out in 1939. Saint-Exupéry enlisted for military service and took part in many dangerous flight missions. After France signed an armistice with Germany in 1940, he traveled to the United States, where Consuelo joined him. For the next two years the couple made their home between New York City, Long Island, and Quebec City, Canada. During this period of exile Saint-Exupéry wrote *Pilote de Guerre* (1942; translated as *Flight to Arras*, 1942), based on a reconnaissance mission he had flown over German territory in 1940 for which he received the Croix de Guerre. Other works written at this time were *Lettre à un Otage* (1943; translated as *Letter to a Hostage*, 1950), and *Le Petit Prince* (*The Little Prince*). Saint-Exupéry also worked on the manuscript for *Citadelle* (*The Wisdom of the Sands*). All these works convey his concern for the spiritual decay that he felt had overtaken Europe and the moral values that he believed were needed for its recovery.

In 1943 Saint-Exupéry sailed for North Africa to rejoin his old flying squadron, stationed at Laghouat, Algeria. At 43, he was told that he was too old for such duties, and he was frequently in pain as a result of his many injuries. He nevertheless insisted on flying high-risk reconnaissance missions from bases in Algeria and Sardinia. He set out from a base on Corsica on his final mission on July 29, 1944. He was reported missing two days later and is believed to have been shot down over Nazi-occupied southern France by a German fighter plane.

In 2004, a French team of underwater researchers found the remains of Saint-Exupéry's plane on the seabed off the coast of Marseille, France. No bullet holes were found, but this may be because the bullet-damaged parts of the plane are still missing.

Chapters One-Three

The Little Prince opens with the narrator recalling a time when he was six years old. He draws a picture, called drawing No. 1. When he shows it to adults, they believe it to represent a hat, whereas the narrator means it to represent a boa constrictor digesting an elephant. He does another drawing, this time clearly showing the elephant inside the boa, but the adults are unimpressed. Discouraged, when he grows up, he learns to fly airplanes. He flies all over the world and meets many adults, but his opinion of them as people of poor understanding does not improve.

The narrator recalls a time six years ago, when his plane's engine failed and he crashed in the Sahara desert. The action jumps back six years. The narrator knows that he must repair the engine quickly, as he only has enough water for a week. On his first night in the desert, he is awakened by a voice asking him to draw a sheep. He is astonished to see a boy standing in front of him. He does not know how to draw a sheep, so repeats drawing No. 1. The boy knows what it is, but he rejects it because elephants and boas are unsuitable for the land where he comes from, where everything is small. The boy rejects the narrator's first three drawings of sheep because the sheep is too sick, has horns, or is old. Impatient to get on with his engine repair, the narrator draws a box with air holes in the side and tells the boy that the sheep is inside. The boy is delighted. The narrator identifies the boy as the little prince of the novel's title.

The prince is amused to hear that, like him, the narrator dropped from the sky. The narrator discovers that the prince comes from another planet. The narrator offers to provide a rope and post to tie up the sheep, but the prince says that this is unnecessary, as his planet is so small that the sheep would have nowhere to go.

Chapters Four-Six

The prince's planet is an asteroid called B-612. The asteroid was identified by a Turkish astronomer, who announced his discovery at an international conference. But because the astronomer was dressed in Turkish attire, no one believed him. Years later, the astronomer repeated his discovery, this time dressed in a Western suit, and was believed.

The narrator says that he has given the name of the prince's planet only because it will make adults believe that the little prince existed. If he were to tell them the important things about the prince, such as that he laughed and wanted a drawing of a sheep, they would dismiss the story.

The narrative jumps forward in time to six years after the narrator and the prince have parted company. The narrator grieves the loss of his friend;

he is writing this story so as not to forget him. He thinks he may make mistakes, as he is getting old and, unlike the prince, cannot see sheep through boxes.

The narrative jumps back to a time when the narrator and the prince are discussing the prince's planet. The prince is pleased that sheep eat shrubs, as his planet's soil is infested with the seeds of baobab trees. Each morning, the prince pulls out the shoots when they are still small, as otherwise they would take over the planet. The prince points out that some jobs are so important that they must not be put off.

The prince enjoys watching sunsets, especially when he is sad. His own planet is so small that he only needs to shift his chair a few inches to see a succession of sunsets.

Chapters Seven-Nine

The prince wants to know whether sheep eat flowers with thorns. The narrator replies that thorns are no defense against being eaten by sheep. He adds that flowers grow thorns out of spite but then admits that he said this only because he is preoccupied with repairing his engine: "I am busy with serious matters." The prince angrily accuses the narrator of being confused. He says that the question of whether sheep eat flowers is vital because on his planet is a flower that is unique, yet it may be destroyed by a sheep in one bite. He says that if someone loves a flower that lives on one star among millions, that is enough to make him happy when he looks at the stars. But if the sheep eats the flower, it is as if "all the stars went dark!" The prince is overcome with tears. The narrator comforts him with a promise to draw a muzzle for his sheep and a fence for his flower.

Media Adaptations

- *The Little Prince* was adapted as a 1974 musical film of the same title with lyrics by Alan Jay Lerner and music by Frederick Loewe. The film, which was directed by Stanley Donen and starred Richard Kiley and Steven Warner, was distributed by Paramount Pictures. It was released on DVD in 2004.

- *The Adventures of The Little Prince —The Complete Animated Series* is a collection on DVD of a 1982 children's television cartoon series loosely based on Saint-Exupéry's novel. It stars the voices of Hal Smith and Julie McWhirter and was released in 2005 by Koch Vision.

- *The Little Prince* was adapted as an opera of the same title by the composer Rachel Portman, with a libretto by Nicholas Wright. A DVD of a staged version of the opera, directed by Francesca Zambello and produced by the BBC as part of its Concert Opera series, was released by Sony in 2005. The production starts Teddy Tahu Rhodes and Joseph McManners.

The prince tells the story of the rose that lives on his planet. As soon as she came into bloom the prince was struck by her beauty, though she was demanding and vain. He looked after her every need, watering her and shielding her from drafts. One day, he caught her telling a trivial lie and began to doubt her. However, the prince now feels that he was foolish to have taken her words seriously. He should have simply admired her and enjoyed her fragrance. He should have recognized the affection behind her tricks.

The narrator speculates that the prince escaped from his planet with the help of migrating birds.

At the beginning of chapter nine, the narrative

point of view shifts to that of the prince. On the morning of his departure, the prince had cleaned out his volcanoes and torn out the baobab shoots. He believes he will not return. As he sadly says goodbye to the flower, she asks him to forgive her for having been silly. She tells him that she loves him, but that as he has decided to leave, he must do so immediately.

Chapters Ten-Twelve

The prince visits several different asteroids. The first is inhabited only by a king who is full of his own importance, in spite of the fact that he has no subjects to rule. He cannot accept that anything should happen unless it is as a result of his orders. The prince wants to leave, so he suggests that the king order him to do so. The prince reflects that grown-ups are odd.

The second planet that the prince visits is inhabited by a conceited man who cares only about being admired. However, as there is no one else on the planet, he never receives any admiration. To humor the man, the prince voices admiration, while thinking, again, that grown-ups are odd.

The third planet that the prince visits is inhabited by a drunkard. The man tells the prince that he drinks to forget that he is ashamed of drinking. The prince feels sad, and concludes once more that grown-ups are odd.

Chapters Thirteen-Fifteen

The fourth planet is inhabited by a businessman who, like the narrator when he meets the prince, is convinced that he is occupied with serious matters. He spends all his time counting the stars, which he thinks he owns. When the prince points out that the businessman cannot pick the stars as one can pick a flower, the businessman says he can put them in the bank. This means that he writes down the number of stars that he owns on a piece of paper and locks it in a drawer.

The prince feels that this is pointless. He himself owns a flower that he waters and volcanoes that he cleans out, so he is of use to the flower and the volcanoes. But the businessman's activities are of no use to the stars. The prince reflects that grown-ups are odd.

On the fifth planet lives a lamplighter whose sole occupation is to light a lamp at dusk and put it out at dawn. He is following orders to do this. Once, it was a reasonable job because the planet's rotation was slow enough to enable him to sleep for the hours between tasks. But now the planet's movement has sped up to one rotation per minute, yet the orders have not changed, so he gets no rest. The prince admires the lamplighter's faithfulness to orders. He reflects that of all the people he has met on his travels, he alone does not appear ridiculous, because he is not concerned only with himself.

The sixth planet is inhabited by a geographer who records in a book the location of the natural features of a land. He knows nothing at all about his own planet, which, the prince has noticed, is rich in natural features. The geographer feels that he is too important to leave his office and do any exploring. Instead, he relies on explorers to come and report their findings.

The prince tells the geographer that the most beautiful thing on his own planet is a flower, but the geographer discounts this as geographies take no account of ephemeral (temporary) things like flowers. The prince is shocked to realize that even though his flower is ephemeral, he has left her alone.

The geographer advises the prince to visit Earth.

Chapters Sixteen-Eighteen

At the beginning of chapter sixteen, the narrative point of view shifts back to the narrator as he gives some facts and figures (presumably for the benefit of those adults who like figures) about the numbers of lamplighters, drunkards, and so forth who live on the seventh planet that the prince visits, Earth.

The narrator says that even though people convince themselves that they take up a lot of space on Earth, if one were to collect them together, the space that they occupied would be tiny.

The narrative point of view shifts to the prince as he arrives on Earth. He lands in the desert. The first creature that he encounters is a snake. The snake says that he is so powerful that he can send a person back to the earth from whence they came simply with a touch. The snake is referring to his power to kill people with his venomous bite. He tells the prince that if he becomes homesick for his planet, he (the snake) can send him back there. The prince knows that the snake is offering to kill him and asks why he speaks in riddles. The snake replies that he also solves them.

The prince asks a flower where he can find people. She says that some passed several years ago. As they have no roots, the wind blows them around.

Chapters Nineteen-Twenty-one

The prince climbs a mountain and calls out a greeting, but hears only his echo in response. Feeling lonely, he fondly remembers that on his own planet, the flower was always the first to speak.

He walks through the desert and finds a garden of roses. He feels disappointed that his rose, contrary to her claim, is not unique.

Chapter twenty-one is the most important chapter in the novel. The prince meets a fox and invites him to play. The fox explains that he cannot, as he is not tame. To tame someone, the fox explains, means to establish ties. If the prince tames the fox, they will need one another and be unique to one another. The prince realizes that his flower has tamed him. The fox says that his life is monotonous, as it consists of hunting chickens and being hunted by men. All chickens are alike and all men are alike, but if the prince tames the fox, they will become unique to one another. The world will have meaning, because everything that reminds each of the other will be a source of joy. Men have no friends, says the fox, because they do not invest the necessary time. They prefer to buy ready-made things at stores.

The fox teaches the prince how to tame him. The prince must approach him gradually and without words, as "words are a source of misunderstandings." Each day the prince must sit a little closer to him, and he must come at the same time each day so that the fox begins to look forward to his visits and can prepare his heart. The fox says this regularity makes their meeting a rite, which he defines as something that makes one day different from all the other days.

The prince tames the fox, but he feels tearful when the time comes to depart. The fox says that this is the price of taming (establishing ties). The fox is glad that the prince tamed him, because each time he sees a golden wheat field he will think of the prince, who has golden hair. He tells the prince to go and look again at the garden of roses. The prince does so and realizes that his rose is unique because he has tamed her by looking after her.

Before the prince leaves, the fox tells him, "It is only with one's heart that one can see clearly. What is essential is invisible to the eye." He adds that men have forgotten this truth: "For what you have tamed, you become responsible forever." The prince knows that he is responsible for his rose.

Chapters Twenty-two-Twenty-four

The prince meets a railway signalman who organizes the transport of thousands of travelers on trains. He observes that while the people travel this way and that, they are never satisfied with where they are. The prince reflects that only children know what they are looking for.

The prince meets a merchant who sells pills that take away people's thirst. Not having to drink saves them fifty-three minutes a week. The prince comments that if he had that amount of spare time, he would use it to drink fresh water from a spring.

The narrative point of view shifts to the narrator. He has not been able to repair his plane and has run out of water. The prince suggests that they look for a well. The narrator thinks there is no chance of finding one, but sets out with the prince. As they walk, the prince reflects that the stars are beautiful because of a flower that one cannot see, and that the desert is beautiful because of a hidden well. The prince falls asleep and the narrator carries him, musing that the prince's physical body is only a shell, and that what is important is invisible. He is moved by the thought of the prince's loyalty to a flower, and he feels that the image of the rose shines through his whole being. At daybreak, the narrator finds a well.

Chapters Twenty-five-Twenty-seven

The prince and the narrator drink water from the well. It tastes sweet and the narrator feels that it nourishes the heart. The prince says that men can grow thousands of roses yet not find what they are looking for. The narrator adds that they could find it in a single rose or a little water.

The prince reminds the narrator of his promise to provide a muzzle for the sheep. The narrator realizes sadly that the prince is planning to leave. The prince asks the narrator to go back to his plane and work on his engine, and to return tomorrow evening to meet him at the well. The narrator reflects that being tamed carries the risk of grief at the loss of the loved one.

By the following evening, the narrator has fixed his engine. He returns to the well to meet the prince and overhears him asking the snake whether his poison is so effective that he will not suffer for long. The narrator reaches for his gun, but the snake slips away. The narrator takes the prince in his arms. The prince says that he is going home, and that the narrator can go home, too. He comforts the narrator by telling him that from now on, whenever the narrator looks at the stars, he will love them all because one of them will be the prince's. The prince tells the narrator not to return tonight, as it will seem as if the prince is suffering and dying, but this will not be true. The narrator ignores this request and goes to meet the prince. The prince says that where he is going, he cannot take his body, as it is too heavy. It will look like an abandoned shell and is nothing to be upset about. The prince weeps as he explains that he is responsible for his flower. The snake bites him and he dies.

The action jumps forward six years to the time when the narrator is writing his story. He has partly recovered from his sorrow, but knows the prince returned to his planet because his body vanished by morning. The narrator loves to listen to the stars at night, as they sound to him like tinkling bells, which in turn are reminiscent of the prince's laughter. He worries that the prince will not be able to fasten the muzzle onto his sheep, as he forgot to draw the strap. He wonders if the sheep has eaten the flower.

In an epilogue, the narrator reflects that his drawing of the place where the prince appeared on Earth and disappeared is the most beautiful but the saddest landscape. He asks that if the reader ever travels through this landscape and meets a child with golden hair, he should write to the narrator to tell him that the prince has returned.

The Businessman

The businessman believes that he is a "serious" man. He spends all his time counting the stars, which he believes he owns. He writes down the figures and locks them in a drawer, an act that he thinks of as putting them in the bank. This, he believes, makes him a rich man.

The allegorical purpose of this character is to show the emptiness of the accumulation of wealth. It is shown as illusory, in that no one can truly own the stars. It is also shown as futile and selfish, in that money kept in the bank is merely figures on a piece of paper that do no good to anyone. The prince's idea of ownership, watering his flower and cleaning his volcanoes, is what is often called stewardship: taking care of the things and beings within one's sphere of responsibility, for the sake of the greater or common good.

The Conceited Man

The conceited man cares only about being admired. As there is no one else on his planet to admire him, this quality is made to look absurd. The allegorical message of this character is that pride and conceit are futile and foolish.

The Drunkard

The drunkard drinks in order to forget how ashamed he is of drinking; he is trapped in a vicious cycle of addiction. In his portrayal of the drunkard, Saint-Exupéry identifies an important truth about alcoholism and addiction in general.

The Fox

The fox is a wise character who teaches the prince about the importance of establishing ties of love and responsibility with another being, a process that he calls taming. He does this by inviting the prince to tame him. Once the prince has tamed the fox, they become unique to one another and lend meaning to the rest of the world, as different aspects of it remind each of the other. Significantly, the fox appears just as the prince is lamenting the fact that his rose is not unique as there are thousands of others like her. Through his relationship with the fox, the prince learns that his rose is unique to him because he has tamed her. The fox also points out the importance of ritual, which makes one day different from another and thus makes it special. He makes the prince observe a ritual (restricting their encounters to a set time each day) during the taming process.

It is worth noting that Saint-Exupéry makes this wise teacher of the prince a wild animal rather than a human being. This reinforces his message that humans have forgotten the most important things in life.

The Geographer

The geographer's allegorical role is to show the limitations of book learning. Shut up in his office, he is ignorant of the world's beauties because he is only interested in official reports from explorers of natural features that fit his criteria. He is not interested in the most beautiful aspect of the prince's planet, the flower, because it is ephemeral. The geographer is another example of how adults can ignore what is essential and restrict themselves to external matters that bring no joy or meaning to life.

The King

The king's role in the allegory is to show the absurdity of worldly pride, grandeur, and power. He thinks of himself as an absolute monarch, but this notion is exposed as absurd because he has no subjects to rule. He maintains his delusion of authority by ordering people to do what they would already do of their own accord. Another ruse he employs to maintain his sense of power is to ensure that he gives only reasonable orders that are within a person's capability to carry out, though he claims that his motive is kindness.

The allegorical message conveyed by the king may be that although people who find themselves in positions of authority may convince themselves that they are important and powerful, in reality they have little control over anything. Life would go on perfectly well without them.

The Lamplighter

The lamplighter is the only character the prince meets on his travels who he does not think is ridiculous, because he is not only concerned with himself. His lighting and putting out his lamp every minute shows his devotion to following orders correctly.

The allegorical purpose of this character may be to satirize bureaucracy, which can be so inflexible that it does not respond to changing circumstances. A rule that was once appropriate (when the planet's rotation was slower) is now inappropriate (because the planet's rotation has speeded up) and creates suffering for the man who is bound by the rule. The lamplighter himself is also a target of satire, as he faithfully but foolishly continues to follow an outdated rule.

The Little Prince

The prince is an enigmatic visitor to Earth from another planet, the asteroid B-612. While the narrator initially treats him rather dismissively as he is busy trying to repair his plane, he soon learns that the prince has a great deal to teach him and is, in fact, the wiser of the two about what is important in life—that is, matters of the heart. His purity of perception is shown by his ability to recognize what the narrator's drawing No. 1 represents. Innocent, joyful, and inquisitive, yet otherworldly, the prince can be seen as an idealized embodiment of childhood.

The prince is not, however, all-knowing, as is evidenced by his constant questioning of the narrator. He has to learn a lesson about his true feelings for the rose on his planet. While he was with her, he felt irritated, frustrated, and doubtful about her because he had caught her lying to him. Once he has left, he realizes that he should have appreciated her deeds and not focused on her words; he should have paid attention to her essence, rather than her superficial behavior. Thus the prince, like the narrator, has to learn the fox's lesson to the effect that "It is only with one's heart that one can see clearly. What is essential is invisible to the eye." The prince passes on what he has learned about love and life's priorities to the narrator. As a result of the fox's teaching, the prince recognizes that he has a lifelong responsibility to his rose and returns home to his planet, albeit through death.

The Merchant

The merchant sells pills intended to quench thirst, eliminating the need to drink. This saves a person fifty-three minutes per week. The prince comments that if he had that amount of spare time per week, he would choose to spend it drinking water from a spring. The allegorical purpose of the merchant is to satirize time-saving gadgets and technological quick fixes that cost money, add nothing of value to life, and in fact make it poorer.

The Narrator

The narrator is an aviator whose life is changed forever by his encounter with the prince six years before he writes the story. Because he makes the same mistakes as much of humanity, he is easier to relate to than the prince and serves as a kind of everyman in the story. He starts out as an imaginative and artistic child, but soon learns to curb his nature when he finds that adults do not understand his drawings. While his chosen profession of pilot may at first glance seem liberating, his life seems empty and lonely until he meets the prince. He has become trapped in the adult delusion of being "busy with serious matters," while he has lost touch with the profound values and matters of the heart represented by the prince. Just as when he was a child, his own imaginative nature was not understood by adults, now that he is an adult, he is slow to grasp the truths presented to him by the child prince. Whereas the prince learns his lessons instantly and without resistance, the narrator proves less open-hearted, driving the prince to tears of anger on one occasion. Eventually, the narrator learns from the prince that the most important thing in life is the bond of love and responsibility that binds people, creatures, and other beings together. The narrator's major bond of love is with the prince, whereas the prince's major bond is with his flower.

It is possible to interpret the narrator and the prince as two aspects of the narrator: the innocent and creative child on whom he turned his back and the adult who has entered the cage of materialistic and practical adult life.

The Railway Signalman

The railway signalman is responsible for organizing travelers on trains. He says that they are never happy with where they are but travel aimlessly. In the context of the allegory, the railway signalman draws attention to the dissatisfaction and lack of fulfillment that plagues humankind. The outward manifestation may be an internal spiritual restlessness or constant travel on the physical level.

The Rose

The rose is a traditional symbol of femininity and love in literature, and Saint-Exupéry's rose in *The Little Prince* fits firmly into this convention. The rose is vain, naïve, and demanding, expecting the prince to cater to her every whim. She displays inner strength when she realizes that the prince wants to leave, asking his forgiveness and telling him to go. Only when the prince has left does he realize that underneath her foolish ways is genuine love for him.

Although the rose seldom appears in the novel, her presence is felt throughout. The prince's annoyance at her follies prompts him to leave his planet, and she is also the reason he returns. As a result of the fox's teachings, the prince realizes that he loves the rose because of the time he has invested in caring for her and that he has a lifelong responsibility to her.

Many critics and biographers of Saint-Exupéry

see the prince's relationship with his rose as based on the author's stormy relationship with his wife Consuelo. They are encouraged in this interpretation by Consuelo de Saint-Exupéry's memoir, *The Tale of the Rose* (2003), in which she writes that she was the model for the character of the rose.

The Snake

The snake is the most aware character in the novel. He needs nothing and nobody and is confident of his own role. He immediately recognizes the prince's innocence and correctly predicts that he will become homesick for his planet and want to return there.

In the context of the allegory, the snake represents death (recalling the Biblical symbol of the serpent in the Garden of Eden who brings death to Adam and Eve). He knows that he has the ultimate power over life and offers to kill the prince, enabling him to return to the earth from which he came. This seems to be the only way that the prince can return to his planet. The snake speaks in riddles, but says that he can also answer them all. This refers to the finality of death, which could be said to solve all problems by ending life.

Themes

Freedom, Love, and Responsibility

The French author André Gide, in his Preface to Saint-Exupéry's novel *Vol de Nuit* (*Night Flight*), notes that Saint-Exupéry's writings express the "paradoxical truth" that an individual's happiness "lies not in freedom but in the acceptance of a duty." Although superficially, the narrator may appear to be free when he flies around the world unburdened by ties and responsibilities, it becomes clear when he meets the prince that he is actually restricted by his corrupted adult awareness. He is unable to hear the prince's serious question about whether the sheep will eat the flower he loves because, as he says, "I am busy with serious matters," attempting to mend his plane. The prince accuses him of "confusing everything ... mixing everything up." In other words, the prince says that the narrator has got his priorities wrong. The narrator forgets his true duty to another human being in pursuit of a perceived duty to practical matters. A matter of the heart that affects the prince deeply is swept aside, but it does not go away. There are emotional consequences to the narrator's warped priorities: the prince is very upset and the narrator has to comfort him.

As the narrator's affection for the prince grows, he finds that there is a price to pay for allowing love into his heart: he is grief-stricken when he has to part from his friend. This is foreshadowed by the prince's story of his meeting with the fox. The fox warns of the perils of taming, or establishing ties, with another being: "If you tame me, we shall need one another." When it comes time for the prince to leave, the fox says, "Oh! … I shall cry."

The process of taming brings a heavy responsibility. The fox tells the prince: "For what you have tamed, you become responsible forever." As the fox and the prince become responsible to each other forever (in that the happiness of each is dependent on the other), so the prince learns that he is responsible to his rose forever, and the narrator learns that he is responsible to the prince forever.

Topics for Further Study

- Research the genre of allegory and read at least one allegorical work by another author. Compare and contrast that author's use of allegory with that of Saint-Exupéry in *The Little Prince*. Consider themes, symbolism, and the didactic (instructional) aspects of the works, along with any other aspects you think are relevant. Give an oral presentation on your findings.

- Write your own allegorical poem, story, or play and read or perform it to the class. End by reading aloud a brief paragraph analyzing the values or qualities you have highlighted in your work and say why they are important.

- Look at drawing No. 1 and drawing No. 2 in chapter one of *The Little Prince*. How do these drawings relate to the themes of the novel? Write an essay on your findings.

- The little prince rejects the narrator's first three drawings of a sheep, just as the adults rejected his drawing No. 1. What is the difference between these two rejections and what does it tell the reader? Lead a class discussion on the topic, first presenting your ideas.

- Consider the little prince's visit to the king (chapter ten), the conceited man (chapter eleven), and the businessman (chapter thirteen).

What is the moral lesson of each of these chapters? How do these lessons relate to the rest of the novel? Write an essay on your findings.

- Read an allegorical work written before 1700 and another written in the twentieth or twenty-first century. Research the social, political, and cultural context of each work. Write an essay in which you (a) compare and contrast the values or lessons that each work attempts to inculcate in the reader, and (b) analyze the relevance of those values to the society of the time.

On the positive side, the fox tells the prince that their dependence on one another will lend meaning to their lives. They will look forward to seeing one another, and everything they see that reminds each of the other will evoke joy in their hearts. Thus, although the fox is wild and as free from ties as the narrator at the beginning of the novel, he longs to be tamed by the prince: "I beg of you ... tame me!" Just as the fox will forever be reminded of the prince when he sees a field of golden corn because it is like the prince's golden hair, so the narrator will forever be reminded of the prince when he sees a sky filled with stars, because on one of the stars lives the prince. The moral lesson that can be extracted from the concept of taming is that the particular (the object of love, which is unique in the world) lends meaning to the general (the rest of the world). The loved one becomes a means of connecting the individual to the whole of creation. Establishing ties of love risks making the heart vulnerable to pain and grief, but without such ties, life is bleak and bereft of meaning.

The Innocence of Childhood

From the novel's beginning, a line is drawn between the perception of adults and the perception of children. Adults, or "grown-ups," are portrayed as having a clouded perception that misses the essential aspects of things and warped priorities that convince them that superficial things are important while profound and significant things are irrelevant. This is shown in the adults' failure to see what the narrator's drawing No. 1 represents. Because the elephant is hidden inside the boa constrictor, the adults cannot see it. They see only the outside, superficial aspect of the form, and so mistake it for a hat and dismiss the drawing as insignificant.

The prince, on the other hand, represents an idealized embodiment of childhood. He instantly recognizes drawing No. 1 for what it really is, as he has the ability to see beyond external forms to the essence within. He rejects the drawing for reasons that are so significant in his world that they are matters of life-and-death. A boa constrictor would be too dangerous, and an elephant too large to live on his planet. Thus his decision to reject the drawing is reasonable and sensible, whereas the adults' reaction is illogical and unwise.

Time and again in the novel, the typical adult perception is shown to be lacking, whereas the child's perception is shown to be clear. When the narrator impatiently tells the prince that flowers have thorns out of spite, because he is too preoccupied to pay attention properly to the subject of flowers and sheep, the prince accuses him of talking "just like grown-ups." He defines what he means: "You are confusing everything … mixing everything up." He tells the story of the man who has "never loved anybody" but "spent all his time adding up figures," all the while convincing himself that he is "busy with serious matters." Such inverted priorities, the prince points out, make a person less than human: "He is not a man, he is a mushroom."

Style

Allegory

The Little Prince is an allegory. Allegory is a narrative technique in which characters represent things or abstract ideas and are used to convey a message or teach a lesson. Allegory is often used to teach moral, ethical, or religious lessons but is sometimes used for satiric or political purposes. Examples of allegorical works include the *Roman de la Rose* (a French poem about love that was originated by Guillaume de Lorris around 1230 and added to by Jean de Meun around 1275), Dante's *Divine Comedy* (written between 1306 and 1321 and first published in 1472) and John Bunyan's *The Pilgrim's Progress* (a Christian allegory published in 1678). The *Roman de la Rose* is linked to *The Little Prince* by the shared symbol of the rose. In the French poem, Rose is both the name of the beloved lady and a symbol of femininity. Similarly, in *The Little Prince*, the rose may be seen both as a character and as a symbol of feminine and romantic love.

In a typical feature of allegory, the characters that the prince meets on his travels each represent a particular human failing. The author's purpose in introducing them is to teach the reader to avoid those failings and to embrace a better way of being, often exemplified by the prince. For example, the character of the businessman shows the futility of accumulating wealth, in that his practice of counting the stars and keeping the records locked in a drawer is obviously a foolish and delusory activity. The function of literature to teach or instruct the reader (usually in moral or spiritual lessons) is called didacticism. The word has its root in the ancient Greek word meaning apt at teaching, *didaktikos*.

The most important teachings of the allegory of *The Little Prince* are voiced by the fox. He teaches the prince the importance of forming bonds of love and responsibility with others and shows him that his main bond of love and responsibility is with his rose, because he has taken care of her.

Symbolism

Fundamental to the allegory, symbolism is a literary device in which concrete objects represent ideas or concepts. Bonner Mitchell, in a 1960 essay for the *French Review* titled "*Le Petit Prince* and *Citadelle*: Two Experiments in the Didactic Style," notes that "virtually everything the hero does, *e.g.* his drinking from a well in the desert, is susceptible of symbolic interpretation; indeed, it obviously requires such interpretation" as otherwise it would have little significance in itself. Mitchell writes that the novel's events are far from realistic and its symbols are correspondingly "obscure in meaning," allowing for individual interpretation.

Prominent symbols in the novel include the well, the rose, the snake, and the prince himself.

The episode (in chapter twenty-five) in which the narrator and the prince drink from the well after a long walk through the desert clearly has a symbolic meaning beyond its literal meaning. This is shown in the narrator's comment that the water was "good for the heart, like a gift," and his associated recollections of childhood Christmases. The water is portrayed as "something entirely different from ordinary nourishment." It is not merely sustenance for the narrator's physical body but is also nourishment for his emotional and spiritual being. The prince adds to the symbolic significance of the episode by commenting that people may grow thousands of roses yet not find that which they are seeking: "And yet, what they are looking for could be found in a single rose or in a little water." He concludes, "But the eyes are blind. One must look with the heart." Thus, drinking from the well that was hidden in the desert becomes symbolic of seeing the invisible spiritual essence of things behind their superficial appearance. The importance of such true vision is one of the novel's central messages.

The rose can be seen as symbolic of love and the feminine. In his relationship with the rose, the prince has to learn to look beyond superficial appearances—her vain and irritating behaviors—to the love and ties of responsibility that, he finally recognizes, underlie them.

The snake is symbolic of death; it has undertones of the Biblical serpent that tempts Adam and Eve and brings death into the Garden of Eden.

The prince has symbolic undertones of Christ that are apparent in his purity and innocence and in the transcendental nature of his death. As with Christ, the prince's appearance on Earth is miraculous, and his departure is equally miraculous. No body is found after his death: it is as if it has been resurrected and accompanied his soul back to his planet.

World War II

Saint-Exupéry wrote *The Little Prince* while living in exile in the United States during World War II. However, attempts to draw parallels between the novel and historical events, such as the character of the snake and the evil of the Holocaust, are unconvincing. What can be said is that Saint-Exupéry's anguish over his exile from his homeland and his feelings about the events taking place appear to have influenced the novel's values. Catharine Savage Brosman, in her essay "Antoine de Saint-Exupéry" for the *Dictionary of Literary Biography*, notes that *The Little Prince* and the other works that the author wrote in exile all "reveal his concern for moral values that, he was persuaded, were essential for the rebuilding of Europe." The moral values exemplified in *The Little Prince* include people's responsibility to their fellows, a sense of the kinship of all humans, and the importance of moral and spiritual values over materialistic interests.

The Vichy Regime

The Vichy regime is the term used to describe the government of France during World War II between July 1940 and 1944. The government was formed by Marshal Philippe Pétain following the military defeat of France by Nazi Germany. Pétain and his government collaborated with the Nazis and even organized raids to capture Jews and other peoples designated by the Nazis to be sent to labor or death camps. The Vichy regime became a source of shame to many French nationals, who saw it as a betrayal of the French people, Jews, and other nations fighting the Nazis.

Saint-Exupéry's exile to the United States occurred later in the same year in which the Vichy regime was established. In 1942, he made a radio broadcast in which, according to Catharine Savage Brosman in her essay "Antoine de Saint-Exupéry" for the *Dictionary of Literary Biography*, he appealed to French nationals in exile "to go beyond the defeat and the Vichy regime and prepare the future together." The message of *The Little Prince* centers around just such bonds of responsibility and brotherhood.

The Allegory in the Twentieth and Twenty-first Centuries

At the time when Saint-Exupéry wrote *The Little Prince*, the literary genre of allegory was out of fashion. This may be because the didacticism (instructive quality) of allegory fell in popularity along with the acceptance of external and monolithic sources of authority such as the church and the state.

Ironically, World War II, the event that convinced Saint-Exupéry that a strong morality and value system was more needed than ever, played a large role in creating cynicism and loss of faith in the old sources of authority. Some states and churches were seen as creating and collaborating with Nazism and its attendant horrors such as the Holocaust.

Compare & Contrast

- **1940s:** Saint-Exupéry's *The Little Prince* is written as an allegory of the traditional kind, expressing moral and spiritual certainties, at a time when allegory is out of favor.

  Today: Allegory, though a popular genre once more, often operates within the demands of realism and frequently expresses moral relativism (a school of thought that holds that morals do not reflect universal truths) or subverts institutions and ideologies.

- **1940s:** After World War II ends in 1945, shortages of basic supplies and consumer goods affect Europe, which may help to prompt an upsurge in materialism. The atrocities of the war lead artists, writers, and philosophers to question long-held beliefs about humanity, God, morality, and progress.

Today: While materialism dominates Western culture, its future is in doubt due to financial and environmental crises. Some forms of religion and spirituality are undergoing a revival.

- **1940s:** The events of World War II lead to the formation of the United Nations in 1945 to facilitate progress toward world peace and social and economic progress.

Today: The War on Terror, religious and ideological conflicts, and uncertainty about the sustainability of the economic system undermine the ideals of social unity and progress.

With the decline in respect for established authorities came a rejection of organized religion and a corresponding rise in individualism, materialism, consumerism, and moral relativism. Moral relativism is a philosophical stance to the effect that moral or ethical values are not objective and universal truths but are instead dependent on changing factors such as social, cultural, or personal circumstances. In practice, this stance manifests as the assumption that an action that is morally right for one person in one situation and at one time may not be morally right for another person in another situation at a different time.

The rise of moral relativism had its counterpart in the field of literature. Allegories written after World War II take more account of the requirements of realism than traditional allegories. They are more likely to have well-developed characters who do not simply stand for a particular quality but have many facets. They are less likely to be dogmatic about what is right and wrong, with characters and situations that reflect moral complexities. In the latter half of the twentieth century, allegories that point to universal truths or uphold political or ideological institutions fell out of favor and were superseded by allegories that undermine these conventional authorities.

Twentieth-century allegorical works that fit the iconoclastic model include political allegories such as George Orwell's novel *Animal Farm* (1945), Hugh Leonard's play *The Au Pair Man* (1968), and J. M. Coetzee's novel *Waiting for the Barbarians* (1980). An allegory on religious and ideological themes is the Egyptian author Najib Mahfuz's novel *Awlad Haratina* (1959), English translations of which were published as *Children of Gebelawi* (1981) and *Children of the Alley* (1996).

Some allegories of this period, such as Paulo Coelho's popular novel *The Alchemist* (first published as *O Alquimista* in 1988 in a Portuguese-language version), do emphasize the importance of spiritual values. But unlike many allegories of the past, which pointed to an externalized set of spiritual or religious values, *The Alchemist* highlights a more modern, subjective, and individualistic type of spirituality that is perhaps best summarized as an injunction to follow one's dream.

In the first decade of the twenty-first century, attitudes appear to have come full circle. The collapse of financial institutions, a growing awareness of corruption in business and politics, and moral outrage at the human cost of military interventions across the globe have prompted intellectuals and politicians to call for a return to a universal system of morals and values.

Critical Overview

The Little Prince is frequently termed a children's story for adults. This fanciful tale of an aviator meeting a prince from another planet in the desert may appeal to children, but other aspects of the story are more likely to appeal to an adult sensibility. These include the tale's moral and spiritual didacticism and the point of view from which it is written—that of an adult nostalgically looking back at the largely lost innocence and wonder of childhood.

The critic Philip A. Wadsworth, in his 1951 essay "Saint-Exupéry, Artist and Humanist" for *Modern Language Quarterly*, notes this dual aspect of the novel and links it, as many critics have done since, to Saint-Exupéry's own life and character. Saint-Exupéry, Wadsworth writes, "refused to turn into a 'grown-up.'" Inside the adult man was always the child, and the book that "most frankly expresses his personality," in Wadsworth's view, is *The Little Prince*, "with its mixture of gaiety and melancholy, of childish fancy and the wisdom of age."

Bonner Mitchell, in an essay for the *French Review* titled "*Le Petit Prince* and *Citadelle*: Two Experiments in the Didactic Style," places Saint-Exupéry's novel firmly in "an illustrious line of allegorical fairy tales which reached its French apogee in the eighteenth-century *conte philosophique* [philosophical tale]." The novel, writes Mitchell, fits less into a contemporary literary genre than into the literature of the past. Mitchell notes the novel's similarity to the *Divine Comedy*, an allegorical epic poem written by the Italian author Dante between 1306 and 1321 and first published in 1472. Mitchell points out that the novel's main message is not contained in the narrator's own remarks: instead, it "must be sought in the actual events and characters which he describes." The book's didacticism is thus "superficially covered over." Moreover, the hero, the prince, is not consciously instructive, although his remarks do indirectly teach the narrator. Similarly, Mitchell writes, the novel's symbolism is also obscure and open to interpretation.

Nona Balakian, in her 1970 review of a biography of Saint-Exupéry for the *New York Times* titled "Poet of the Air—and Earth," makes a general comment about the author that could apply to *The Little Prince*. Balakian writes that the author "breathed the romance of the air as no one had done before or has since." Nonetheless, she adds, the adventures he most prized were "those that had to do with the earth, with the world of men and their immutable link to each other."

Robert Gibson is one of many critics who explores the many correspondences between the novel and Saint-Exupéry's life and experiences. In his 1995 essay for the *Reference Guide to World Literature*, "Antoine de Saint-Exupéry: Overview," Gibson points out that Saint-Exupéry wrote the book when he was living in exile in the United

States, "cut off from both the country and the people he most loved." In line with this period of the author's life, Gibson notes, the novel has been variously interpreted as "a hymn of exile and a lament for lost innocence."

The Little Prince has enjoyed great popularity with the public. Judy Quinn, in an article for *Publishers Weekly*, writes that as of 2000, the book had become available in sixty-two countries and had been translated into ninety-five languages, and it was still selling nearly 200,000 copies per year.

A key to its enduring popularity is suggested by Rachel Lynn Strongheart in an article for the *Reading Teacher* called "The Little Prince: My Ally from Asteroid B-612" (2001). Strongheart writes that of all the books she encountered as a child, "it best embodies and safeguards the magic I felt and believed in as a child." Strongheart sees strong correspondences between the trials of her own life and those of the stranded pilot in the novel. Always concerned with "matters of consequence," she feels trapped in "that self-imposed cage of practicality that ignores the heart and withers creativity." Only the wisdom of the little prince, she writes, "allows a smile or kind word to take precedence over my ever-present and ever-growing list of things to do."

What Do I Read Next?

- Antoine de Saint-Exupéry's novel *Vol de Nuit* (1931; translated into English as *Night Flight*, 1932), is widely viewed as a classic of aviation. It tells the story of the men who risked their lives in pioneering the airmail service by flying planes over South America and the managers who gave the orders.

- The French philosopher and author Voltaire's *Candide* (1759) is an allegorical and satirical novel that tells the story of the trials of the young Candide and his mentor Dr. Pangloss. Voltaire's satirical targets include the naïve optimism promoted by the German philosopher Gottfried Wilhelm

Leibniz, along with romantic love, science, philosophy, religion, and government.

- Allegory is not only a literary genre; it is also used in the visual arts. Matilde Battistini's *Symbols and Allegories in Art* (2005) is a fascinating book that breaks down various famous works of art into their component parts and explains the allegorical and symbolic meanings of each.

- Louis S. Rehr's *Marauder:Memoir of a B-26 Pilot in Europe in World War II* (2003) is a compelling account of Rehr's war experience from a Midwestern military academy in the United States, to pilot training, to joining a squadron in Europe, to the end of the war as commander of the squadron.

Sources

Balakian, Nona, "Poet of the Air—and Earth," in the *New York Times*, December 5, 1970, p. 30.

Brosman, Catharine Savage, "Antoine de Saint-Exupéry," in *Dictionary of Literary Biography*, Vol. 72, *French Novelists, 1930-1960*, edited by Catharine Savage Brosman, Gale Research, 1988, pp. 314-30.

Gibson, Robert, "Antoine de Saint-Exupéry: Overview," in the *Reference Guide to World Literature*, 2nd ed., edited by Lesley Henderson, St. James Press, 1995.

Gide, André, "Preface," in *Vol de Nuit*, by Antoine de Saint-Exupéry, 1931, reprint, Ebooks Libres et Gratuits, May 2004, p. 5, http://www.scribd.com/doc/2324523/Vol-de-nuit?autodown=pdf (accessed November 29, 2008).

Mitchell, Bonner, "*Le Petit Prince* and *Citadelle*: Two Experiments in the Didactic Style," in the *French Review*, April 1960, pp. 454-61.

Quinn, Judy, "'Prince' and the Revolution," in *Publishers Weekly*, Vol. 247, No. 11, March 13, 2000, p. 26.

Saint-Exupéry, Antoine de, *The Little Prince*, translated by Irene Testot-Ferry, Wordsworth Classics, 1995.

Strongheart, Rachel Lynn, "The Little Prince: My

Ally from Asteroid B-612," in the *Reading Teacher*, Vol. 54, No. 5, February 2001, p. 498.

Wadsworth, Philip A., "Saint-Exupéry, Artist and Humanist," in *Modern Language Quarterly*, March 1951, pp. 96-107.

Further Reading

Bloomfield, Morton W., ed., *Allegory, Myth, and Symbol*, Harvard University Press, 1981.

> This book is a useful collection of essays by different critics analyzing the use of allegory, myth, and symbol in a variety of works from the Anglo-Saxon era to the poetry of W. B. Yeats, Ezra Pound, and T. S. Eliot.

Grant, R. G., *Flight: 100 Years of Aviation*, DK, 2007.

> This large volume was produced in collaboration with the Smithsonian Institution's National Air and Space Museum. The book traces the history of aviation through its innovations, adventures, and pioneers and is lavishly illustrated with archival photographs.

Quilligan, Maureen, *The Language of Allegory: Defining the Genre*, Cornell University Press, 1992.

> This book provides a critical analysis of allegories both ancient and modern.

Robinson, Joy Marie, *Antoine de Saint-Exupéry*, Twayne's World Authors Series, Twayne Publishers, 1984.

This book offers an accessible and concise critical introduction to the author's works along with biographical material and resources for further study.

Saint-Exupéry, Consuelo de, *The Tale of the Rose*, Random House, 2003.

Saint-Exupéry's widow Consuelo wrote this compelling memoir of their tempestuous marriage in 1945, a year after his death. The manuscript languished in a trunk for decades until it was discovered in 1999. Consuelo describes how she was the model for the character of the rose in *The Little Prince*.

Schiff, Stacy, *Saint-Exupéry: A Biography*, Holt Paperbacks, 2006.

This is a very readable biography by a Pulitzer Prize-winning author. Readers will enjoy spotting the many parallels between the otherworldly aviator Saint-Exupéry and the two protagonists of his novel *The Little Prince*.

CPSIA information can be obtained
at www.ICGtesting.com
Printed in the USA
BVHW09s1735111018
529909BV00003B/1172/P